Previously ...   4

Episode 1
Changing Places   6

Episode 2
The American Patient   12

Episode 3
The Commitments   18

Episode 4
So you wanna be a rock'n'roll star?   24

Episode 5
Band on the Run   29

Episode 6
The Show Must Go On   35

Resource Bank   43

Pairwork   49

Transcript   51

Meet the characters.

Previously ...

PART ONE

JANE

DAVID

SIMON

HELEN

MATT

1 Watch ≫ the video up to the kiss and hug.

Write the names of the characters in the order they appear.

1 ....

2 ....

....

....

3 ....

2 Where do you see them? Tick (✔) the names of the people you see in these different places.

	JANE	DAVID	SIMON	HELEN	MATT
on the doorstep					
in the street					
by the car					
in the living-room					
next to the computer					
by the river					

Watch ≫ again and check.

PART TWO

ALI

EDDIE

BILL

1 **What do you think?**
Here are some more characters in the story. What do you think their relationship with Jane , Helen, Simon, David and Matt could be?

2 Watch ➤ the rest of the video montage.

a) Who comes down the steps and greets Jane? ....

b) Who picks up some flowers? ....

c) Who throws his arms in the air? ....

d) Who is in the car with Jane? ....

e) Who gives a 'high five' to Jane? ....

Episode 1

Changing Places

Before you watch

1 Look at the advert then answer the questions.

House for rent
Central Oxford

Beautiful two-bedroom flat in Georgian town house with lovely garden and ample parking. All modern appliances. Near city centre. Friendly landlord. Two hundred quid a week (Cash only). Non-smokers. No pets. Professionals preferred. Phone: **Steady Eddie Properties** on Oxford 425555 (office hours only)

a) How many bedrooms are there?

b) Is there a garden?

c) How much is the rent?

d) Can you have a dog?

e) Can students apply?

2 Get into pairs. Ask and answer these questions.

- Where do you live?

- What's your idea of the perfect place to live?

- Have you ever moved house?

- Why do people move house?

- What's difficult about moving house?

- What's fun about moving house?

- Why do people move out of their parents' house?

3 What do you think?
Imagine you are going to Oxford with some friends to study English.

- Would you be interested in renting this house? Why / Why not?

While you watch

Let me give you a hand

SECTION ONE

(up to **Bill**: *So, can you try to keep the noise down?*)

Moving

1 Watch ⟩ section one and answer the questions. Tick (✔) the correct box.

a) Jane is moving ...

   in. ☑   out. ☐

b) Jane is in the ...

   kitchen. ☐   living-room. ☑

c) What does Eddie help Ali with?

   a television ☐   a lamp ☑

d) Jane moved out because she wanted ...

   more space. ☑   a change. ☑

e) Matt was going out with ...

   Helen. ☐   Jane. ☑

f) They drop the ...

   lamp. ☐   television. ☑

g) What time is it?

   3 p.m. ☐   2 p.m. ☑

h) Bill, the neighbour, has just got back from ...

   New York. ☑   Los Angeles. ☐

2 Before you watch again, complete the questions with the correct verb form in the box.

isn't ✓	is ✓	can ✓	did ✓	can't ✓
	do ✓	's	did ✓	is ✓

a) Where ...*do*... you want this chair, Jane?

b) What ...*did*... you say the neighbours were like?

c) Why ...*did*... you want to move in here?

d) ...*is*... it reliable?

e) That's not really the basis for a relationship, ...*is*... it?

f) ...*isn't*... there a 24-hour emergency service?

g) What the hell ...*is*... going on down there?

h) Well, ...*can't*... you move in some other time?

i) So, ...*can*... you try to keep the noise down?

Now watch ⟩ **again and check.**

(up to **Eddie:** *That's beyond repair, mate.*)

The music business

1 Eddie asks Matt and Jane some questions. Before you watch, predict their replies.

a) Is this your guitar, Jane?

b) Are you in a band?

c) Have you got any gigs planned?

d) Has your band made a CD?

Now watch ⫸ and check.

Eddie doesn't ask one of the questions. Which one is it?

2 Read the sentences. Then watch ⫸ and change any information that is incorrect.

a) Matt has just been to a rehearsal with his band.

b) Jane didn't know Matt was in a band.

c) Matt's band hasn't played any gigs yet.

d) Eddie has worked with *Led Zeppelin*, *Deep Purple* and *The Beatles*.

e) Eddie thinks the television is easy to repair.

3 What do you think?

• How good do you think Matt's band is?

• What type of music do you think they play?

(up to **Matt:** *Please, David. It's important. Please!*)

The ideal flatmate

1 Who would you share a house with?

Tick (✔) the 3 or 4 qualities which you think are important in a flatmate from the list below.

	You	The friends
non-smoker	✓	✓
interesting	✓	
friendly	✓	✓
clean	✓	
rich		
good sense of humour	✓	
good taste in music	✓	
male		
female	✓	
good-looking	✓	
quiet	✓	✓
similar age		
professional		✓

Now watch ⧁ and tick the qualities the friends consider important. Are they the same as yours or different?

2 Here is the conversation between the friends. Change the words in italics to the words actually used in the video.

Helen: Professional.

David: Non-smoking.

Helen: *Yes.* a) .... What else was in the advert when you moved in?

Ali: Here you are.

Helen: Oh, thanks, Ali.

David: Thanks.

Helen: What time do you finish today?

Ali: At six. Are you all coming to see our new flat?

Helen: *Yes.* b) ....

David: *Yes, of course.* c) ....

Ali: Great.

Jane: Quiet.

Helen: That's important. Put that in. What is it, David?

David: What? Oh, nothing. *I'm going to the toilet.*
   d) .... What's going on?

Matt: Have you got any money?

David: Money? How much? *I think I can give you five pounds.*
   e) ....

Matt: Two hundred.

David: Two hundred pounds! You must be joking! *Why*
   f) .... do you want two hundred pounds?

Matt: Please, David. It's important. Please!

Check your answers with the transcript on page 51.

SECTION FOUR

(to the end of the episode)

House warming

1 Someone is going to give Ali and Jane these presents. Who do you think each one is from? Draw a line to the person you think it is.

MATT   EDDIE   BILL   SIMON

Now watch ⟩ section four and check your ideas.

2 Now watch ⟩ again. Tick (✔) the correct answer.

a) Ali thinks the rent is ...

   cheap. ☐   reasonable. ☐   expensive. ✔

b) How does Helen feel about her relationship with Simon?

   confident ☐   angry ☐   unsure ✔

c) Who said that the television was very expensive?

   Ali ☐   David ✔   Matt ☐

d) Bill was rude earlier because he was ...

   jet-lagged. ✔   ill. ☐   studying. ☐

e) Bill is ...

   Australian. ☐   South African. ☐

   American. ✔

REVIEW

The characters

Note down what you have learned about the characters on the cards below.

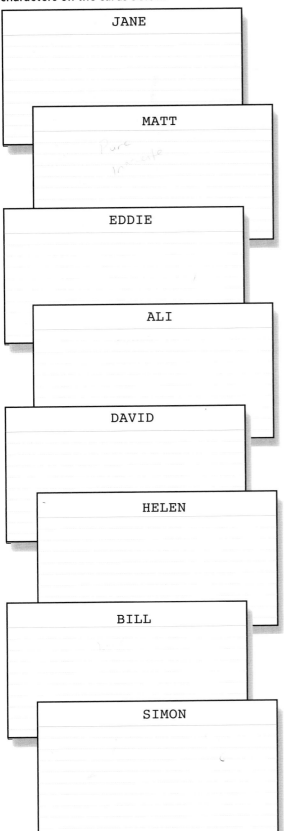

JANE

MATT

Pure lunatic

EDDIE

ALI

DAVID

HELEN

BILL

SIMON

After you watch

1 What do you think?

- Which of the characters in the episode would you prefer to share a flat with?

- What do you think about these relationships?

a) Simon and Helen   b) Matt and Jane

- Which characters would make a good couple? Why?

Role play

2 The situation

Before Ali and Jane moved in, Eddie Usher showed the house to many other people.

Work in groups of three.

Students A and B: You are the prospective tenants. Find out as much information as you can about the following aspects of the flat. Be persistent! Use these notes to plan your questions.

Things to ask:

- What / neighbours / like?
- Where / park / car?
- Which / shops / near the flat?
- What kind / heating / in flat?
- Price / include / bills?
- What / public transport?

- How far / centre / city?
- Phone / in house?
- What / do / in emergency?
- Deposit? How much?
- ....?
- ....?

Student C: Turn to page 49, Pairwork.

Episode 2
The American Patient

Before you watch

1 What do you think?
Work in groups, A or B .

Group A

What annoys you the most?
Choose three things.

- When somebody is late.

- When two people are talking at the same time.

- Loud traffic noise.

- When a TV in a café is on too loud.

- When you just miss a bus or train.

- When somebody is rude to you.

- Things that are unfair.

- People talking loudly in cinemas.

Group B

What embarrasses you the most?
Choose three things.

- When your mobile phone rings in the cinema.

- When you call somebody by the wrong name.

- When you forget somebody's birthday.

- When you turn up late.

- When you forget to zip up your jeans.

- When somebody gives you a big compliment.

- When you make a mistake.

- When you have an argument in public.

2 Form a pair with someone from the other group and share your opinions.

3 Why do you think ...

... Helen gets annoyed?

... Jane gets embarrassed?

While you watch

(up to **Helen:** *Take last Tuesday ...*)

Down in the dumps

1 Watch ⟫ section one and answer the questions about Helen. Tick (✔) the correct answer.

a) Where is Helen?

at work ☐ in the café ☑ at home ☐

b) What is she doing?

making a call ☐ sending an SMS ☑

drinking an orange juice ☐

c) Jane is late. What is Helen's reaction?

She is angry. ☐ She starts crying. ☐

She doesn't mind. ☑

d) Who does Helen talk about first?

Simon ☐ Matt ☐ Jane ☑

e) How is she feeling?

hungry ☐ depressed ☑ angry ☐

2 Helen says that Matt has changed. Watch ⟫ the second half of section one again and note down these changes.

Before
quiet
sleep

Now
noisy
take the quieter

SECTION TWO

(up to **Helen:** ... *someone else.*)

At the cinema

1 Watch  section two. Are these statements true (T) or false (F)?

    a) Helen is waiting for Simon.   T

    b) Simon is on time.   F

    c) Helen's phone rings.   F

    d) They leave together.   F

    e) Helen is angry with Simon.   T

2 What happened? Number the statements below in the right order 1 to 6. The first has been given.

    a) 4   Somebody telephoned Simon.

    b) 5   This situation has been happening a lot recently.

    c) 1   She waited for more than half an hour outside the cinema.

    d) 6   She thinks he has another girlfriend.

    e) 3   The film started.

    f) 2   He arrived.

Now watch  and check.

3 Circle the correct verb tense to retell Helen's story.

Now watch  again and check.

> I *was waiting* / *had been waiting* outside the cinema for over half an hour before he *turned up* / *had turned up*. I *looked forward* / *was really looking forward* to seeing this film but it *had only just started* / *has only just started* when his mobile *had rung* / *rang*. It *has been* / *is* like this for weeks ... I think he *sees* / *is seeing* someone else.

4 What do you think?

• Does Simon have another girlfriend? If not, why is he acting so strangely?

(up to **Bill**: *Can you hear me?*)

Doors and floors

1 Watch ⟩ the first part of section three (up to **Jane**: *I decided to have a shower*) and then note down 10 things in Jane and Ali's living-room.

1 ...backKianaic...   6 ...sofa...

2 ...the wallet...nice... 7 ...vase...

3 ...decides...screaming... 8 ...box...

4 ...another...   9 ....

5 ...tea...   10 ....

Now watch ⟩ again and check.

2 **With sound only**, listen ⟩ to the rest of section three. After Jane leaves the living-room, what do you think happened?

Check your predictions with a partner. Now watch ⟩ **with pictures and sound** to see what actually happened.

3 Now watch ⟩ again and fill in the spaces with the correct verb form.

After Jane ...had tidied... (tidy) the flat, she ...decided... (decide) to

have a shower so she ...went... (go) into the bathroom and

...closed... (close) the bathroom door. Bill ...was coming... (come)

down the stairs when he ...heard... (hear) a scream. He

...ran... (run) down the stairs and ...banged... (bang) on the

door. The phone ...rang... (ring) so Jane ...came... (come)

out of the bathroom. As she ...was running... (run) to answer the phone, she

...stubbed... (stub) her toe and ...screamed... (scream). Bill

...broke... (break) the door down and ...ran... (run) into the

living-room where Jane ...was lying... (lie) on the floor.

(to the end of the episode)

Sparks fly

1 Watch ⟫ the final section and answer the questions.

a) How many times did Bill have to remind Jane to turn the electricity off? 2

b) What happened when she was on her way to do this?
   Phone was ring

c) What did she do next? Answ the phone

d) Who did she talk to? Helen

e) What happened to Bill?

2 Now match these questions with the correct answer.

a) Can you turn off the mains switch? ●

b) What are you up to? ●

c) Can we talk? ●

d) Shall I come and meet you there, say, in half an hour? ●

e) What is that stuff? ●

f) Is that the guy I saw you with last Sunday? ●

g) Is he your boyfriend? ●

h) And then what happened? ●

1 ● No, ex-boyfriend.

2 ● Yeah.

3 ● Thanks, Jane.

4 ● It's a homeopathic cure.

5 ● Of course.

6 ● Er, yeah.

7 ● Nothing. I came here and left him to mend the door.

8 ● I'm standing outside Freud's and waiting for Simon.

Watch ⟫ again and check.

3 What do you think?

• Which story do you prefer? Why?

• What do you think will happen next ...
  to Helen and Simon?
  to Jane and Bill?

For each of the following lines write:
a) the name of the character who said it,
b) where it was said.

LINES	WHO	WHERE
Matt's changed since you left. He used to be so quiet, asleep most of the time and half-asleep the rest of it. But now he's taken up the guitar.		
Hello mate! Wow! OK. Yeah. I'm really sorry, pet, but I've got to go.		
I've got to hear this! I'll be right back.		
I fancied a relaxing evening, so I made the flat nice and decided to have a shower.		
Is he your boyfriend?		

Watch ⧉ the whole episode again and check.

After you watch

1 At the beginning of the episode, Helen sends this SMS message to Simon.

This is a short way of writing *Where are you Simon?*

Here are some other common abbreviations. In pairs, try and guess what they mean. Then check with other pairs.

abbr.	Meaning	abbr.	Meaning
AFAIK	....	IOW	....
ASAP	....	L8R	....
ATM	....	MTE	....
BTW	....	OIC	....
B4N	....	THX	....
CU	....	U	....
CU L8R	....	U2	....
GR8	....	U4E	....
IC	....	WTG	....
IMO	....	W8	....

Now check with the answers on page 50 Episode 2 of the Pairwork section.

2 Is it love?
Look at the end of the transcript for Episode 2 on page 52. Read the final conversation between Jane and Bill starting with:

Bill: *Hey, take it easy.*

until

Jane: *No ... ex-boyfriend.*

Underline any expressions that show a possible romantic interest between them. Share your expressions with the rest of the class.

Episode 3

The Commitments

Before you watch

1 Match the names and the instruments.

.... guitar   .... keyboards   .... trumpet   .... bass

.... trombone   .... drums   .... piano   .... saxophone

Do you play any of these instruments?
If not, which would you like to learn? Why?

2 Imagine you are going to form your own band. Look at the following qualities and cross out 3 that are not necessary for a successful band.

- To be able to play a musical instrument really well. ✓

- To be good-looking. ✓

- To be available all the time.

- To be determined. ✓

- To have a beautiful smile.

- To be well organized.

- To have fashionable clothes.

- To write good songs. ✓

- To have experience of performing in public.

SECTION ONE

(up to **Eddie:** *I've drawn up a contract for you.*)

Practice makes perfect

1 Watch ⫸ section one. Are these statements true (T) or false (F)?

a) Simon is playing the keyboards. ▢

b) There are four members of the band. ▢

c) They are practising. ▢

d) They are playing jazz music. ▢

e) Eddie has come to join the band. ▢

SECTION TWO

(up to **Bill:** *Sure.*)

Going for a spin

1 Watch ⫸ section two and correct the information.

a) Jane wanted to go for a ride into town.

b) Bill says he will repair the car later.

c) Jane is sure the car is safe.

d) The MG is one of the finest American sports cars ever made.

e) Jane goes inside to have a shower.

2 What did they say? Before you watch again, complete their sentences.

a) Why don't ●   ● fix that for you later.

b) I should stay ●   ● got time to wash my hands?

c) I can ●   ● you come with me?

d) Come ●   ● you coming?

e) So, are ●   ● and sort this out.

f) Have I ●   ● on!

Now watch ⫸ and check.

SECTION THREE

(up to Ali using her mobile phone)

Eddie spells it out

1 Watch ≫ section three. Complete what Eddie says.

a) Ok. ....'s get down to business.

b) I think you boys are good. I even think you ....
become quite big ... if you get the breaks.

c) You .... get a new singer. Got it?

d) Do I.............. to spell it out?

e) Good. Because you .... always listen to your Uncle
Eddie.

Now watch ≫ again and check.

2 What do you think?

- Who is Ali sending a message to?

- What do you think she is writing?

SECTION FOUR

(up to **Jane:** *Hi, Helen. It's Jane.*)

On the road

1 Watch ≫ section four. Are these statements true (T) or false (F)?

a) Jane doesn't like Bill's car.

b) Jane understands everything Bill is saying.

c) Bill's phone rings.

d) Jane receives a message on her phone.

e) Jane phones Matt.

(up to **Eddie**: *You won't regret this.*)

Contact and contract

1 Watch ⊳ the first part of section five (up to **Eddie**: *What do you say?*). Number these sentences 1 to 5 in the order that you hear them.

a) ☐ I can give you boys a helping hand.

b) ☐ I could ask him to come along to your show.

c) ☐ We could set up a gig for ourselves.

d) ☐ You don't have to sign anything you don't want to.

e) ☐ I can fix you up with a gig.

2 Watch ⊳ the second part of section five (up to **Bill**: *The job's good.*). Which of the following were part of Jane's drama training?

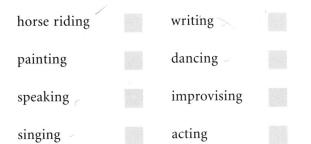

horse riding	☐	writing	☐
painting	☐	dancing	☐
speaking	☐	improvising	☐
singing	☐	acting	☐

3 Put Eddie's words in the correct order to make sentences.

a) need / 's / no / thing / to / whole / there / read / the

....

b) have / here / you / to / just / sign

....

c) signature / only / need / one / we

....

Now watch ⊳ and check.

4 What do you think?

• Should the boys trust Eddie?

• Should they let him become their manager?

(to the end of the episode)

Patching things up

1 **What do you think?**

Watch ≫ section six and draw lines between the pictures of the characters to indicate a relationship which is:

a) beginning.

b) over.

c) back on again.

You can introduce one of the other characters if you wish. Be prepared to justify your choice.

2 Watch ≫ the video and complete the sentences with these words and phrases.

Well	The thing is	You know	You know
Right	You mean	Yeah	

a) .... how Matt's really cut up about Jane.

b) .... all this secrecy was just because of Matt?

c) ...., Eddie thinks it is.

d)..........................., I haven't had this much fun in a long time.

e) ...., I might be going back to the States.

f) ...., the chain keeps coming off.

g) .... I'll see you then. Bye.

Now watch ≫ again and check.

Then label your lines a), b) or c).

REVIEW

Read the summary. It has six mistakes. Correct them.

Eddie came to see the band when they were rehearsing and offered them a gig. They all went to the café to discuss this. Eddie tried to persuade them to sign a contract, indicating what he could do for them and what they had to do to become a better band. In the end, Matt refused to sign the contract. Simon and Helen had an argument.

Bill met Jane when she was relaxing in the garden and invited her to go for a spin in his MG sports car. They went for a drive in town and got to know each other better. Bill told her that he might be going back to the States because of his family.

Now watch ⟩ the whole episode again and check.

After you watch

1 Advice to musicians signing a contract

Read the following text and put in the correct modal verbs (*can*, *should*, etc). The first has been done as an example for you.

Legal advice for musicians

When musicians are offered a contract, they a) **should** always get legal advice first. A contract is a legally binding document between two sides, which b) .... be the artist and a manager, publisher, record company or even between band members. The contract states for example how the manager c) .... be paid and what a band d) .... do – the recordings and concerts, etc. Any document which legally binds you to certain terms and conditions e) .... be completely examined and understood before signing. If the manager says, "you don't f) .... to read the whole thing – it's a standard agreement", make sure you do read the whole thing!

Young adults under 18 g) .... have a parent or guardian sign their contracts, and nothing h) .... be signed without them being present.

Contacts i) .... be a simple one page document or contain many pages, so take your time to read everything carefully. If you don't want to regret signing a terrible contract and you are not sure what the contract means, you j) .... show it to a professional.

(Source: www.vocalist.org.uk/contracts.html)

Episode 4

So you wanna be a rock'n'roll star?

Before you watch

Read the text. Are the statements below true (T) or false (F) ?
If false, justify your answer.

Wherever we go we hear music. Why? Because we love it and we want it. We want it when we drive, eat breakfast, shower, work, shop for stuff — it's the aural landscape of our lives.

We hear music on recordings, at concerts, on TV commercials and at the airport; we listen to music over the phone and in our video games and mobile phones. The global demand for music is chronic and ever-growing.

We're purchasing music just about everywhere too. In the past you bought records at record shops; today you can get them at record shops, supermarkets, chemists, bookshops, consumer electronic superstores, bars, gyms, museum shops, through the mail, over the Internet, at the airport, at McDonald's and hundreds of other places — MUSIC IS EVERYWHERE!

There's a new dynamic in the business today, one that is different from what people previously thought. It can be said the first phase of the music industry (c. 1935-70) was music-driven, new sounds came up from the streets and clubs, and music companies responded.

The second phase (c. 1970-1995) was business-driven — lawyers and accountants ascending to decision-making posts and corporate imperatives dictating "hits".

The third phase (1995-now) seems to be market-driven. Consumers themselves are taking control of their music consumption. There are of course elements of all three approaches at all times, but one has dominated each era.

So bands can still make it but they have to think very carefully what kind of music they wish to make, where they wish to perform, and how they wish to record and distribute their music. The future is uncertain, in a positive way.

a) There are not many places to listen to music.

b) It used to be easier to buy music.

c) The writer thinks there have been three stages in the music industry.

d) Nowadays, bands must only think carefully about their music and where they play.

e) The future can be positive for musicians.

(up to **Matt:** *We're just this way.*)

The future is uncertain

1 Watch  the first part of section one (up to **Ali:** *See you. Bye.*). Tick (✔) the appropriate box.

a) Jane and Bill are going to have a

☐ romantic evening.   ☑ drink.

b) How does Jane feel about a relationship at the moment?

☐ She wants one.   ☑ She doesn't want one.

c) How would Jane feel about a long distance relationship?

☐ positive   ☑ negative

2 What do you think?

- Is Jane saying what she really feels?

3 Watch the second part of section one and number these activities 1 to 7 in the order you see them. The first has been given.

a) 2 Melissa arrives.

b) 4 David phones Matt.

c) 1 David walks around the corner.

d) 3 David asks Melissa for directions.

e) 6 Matt ends the call.

f) 5 Matt opens the door.

g) 7 Matt speaks to Melissa.

Now watch again and check.

4 Watch again and complete the conversation.

David: Oh sorry ... um ... I'm a .... lost. I'm trying to find a rehearsal room ...

Melissa: For 'The Broken Hearts'? Are you going to the audition? You don't look .... a singer.

David: Me? No. I'm a friend. A friend and an adviser. Is that where you're going? I can't find the number.

Melissa: Me neither. I've never .... before.

David: ...., I've got an idea.

Matt: Hello.

David: Matt.

Matt: David! Hi! ...., I'm taking a call ...

David: Matt!

Matt: Oh, right. Come in. For the ....?

Melissa: Yeah.

Matt: Great. ....

Now watch again and check.

SECTION TWO

(up to Melissa singing *Amazing Grace*)

First appearances

1 Watch ⧁ the first part of the section (up to **Matt:** *You're a real mate!*)

Which of the following does David mention? Tick (✔) the boxes.

a) the free advice he's giving Matt ☐

b) Simon is feeling nervous ☐

c) filming the audition ☐

d) the terms of the contract ☐

e) the money he lent Matt ☐

2 What do you think?
Both Iggy and Melissa are auditioning for Matt's band.

- What type of person is Melissa / Iggy?

- What type of music do you think he / she likes?

- What song will they sing to impress Matt and the others?

- Who will be the new singer in Matt's band?

Now watch ⧁ until Melissa starts sing *Amazing Grace*.

3 Complete what Melissa says with either the Present Perfect Simple or the Past Simple.

I .... (always want) to be a singer in a band. In fact, I .... (be) in a band and our records .... (sell) all over the world.

You know, I .... (have) a number 27 hit in Norway, and .... (get) into the top one hundred in Luxembourg. And we .... (be) pretty successful for about two years. But then it all .... (go) wrong. Our manager was sent to prison ... he .... (be) really horrible ... he .... (cheat) us out of lots of money.

Well, I .... (be) eight when I .... (join) the band, so I guess I was ten when we .... (split) up.

Now watch ⧁ and check.

SECTION THREE

(to the end of the episode)

The other side of Bill and Jane

1 What do you think?
In this section, Jane and Ali say the following:

What do you make of that?

He's amazing.

- What or who do you think they could be talking about?

Now watch ▷ and find out.

2 Watch ▷ the first part of section three again (up to **Ali:** *You're always singing at home!*).

Complete what the characters say.

a) **Jane:** We're just two ships .... in the night.

b) **Ali:** Well, I hope you won't be sending me ....!

c) **Simon:** She's .... though!

d) **Helen:** I think we could all .... a drink.

e) **Bill:** Why don't you sing ....?

Now watch ▷ and check.

3 Watch ▷ and listen to the song. At the end of each line, note down who is singing by writing: (B) for Bill, (J) for Jane and (B+J) for both Bill and Jane.

Mustang Sally, guess you'd better slow that mustang down.   *B*

Mustang Sally my baby, guess you'd better slow your mustang down.   *B+J*

You've been running all over town.

I guess you'd better keep your flat feet on the ground.

All you wanna do is ride around, Sally,

ride, Sally, ride.

All you wanna do is ride around, Sally,

ride, Sally, ride.

All you wanna do is ride around, Sally,

ride, Sally, ride.

All you wanna do is ride around, Sally,

ride, Sally, ride.

One of these early mornings,

You're gonna be wiping those weeping eyes.

(c) Sir Mack Rice, EMI Music.

4 What do you think?

- Who is going to be the singer in Matt's band?

- Imagine the band wants two backing vocalists and have asked your class to supply them. Who would be a good choice?

REVIEW

Who said what?

Watch ▶ the whole episode and draw a line between the person and what they said.

DAVID

MELISSA

JANE

MATT

- You don't look much like a singer.

- I normally charge for legal advice, and I doubt that you could afford my hourly rate!

- I'll start paying you back after our gig. You're a real mate!

- I'd like some more information about your acupuncture classes.

- Come off it, Jane! You're crazy about him!

- In an obvious way, that doesn't appeal to me.

- I played in jazz clubs back home. For a time I even thought about going professional.

- I think you've found your singer.

HELEN

BILL

SIMON

ALI

After you watch

1 Matt and Simon are talking on the phone later that day. Replace the words in bold with a more informal equivalent from the box below.

....

| mate | fit | see you |
| hang on | just a minute | quid |

....

Simon: Hi Matt, can you talk?

Matt: Erm ... **wait a moment** a) .... please. OK.

Simon: What did you think of Melissa?

Matt: Well, she can't sing ...

Simon: ... but she is really **attractive** b) .... !

Matt: Honestly! And you've got a girlfriend! I've got more to worry about though.

Simon: Why? What's up?

Matt: It's David. He's a really good **friend** c) .... , and he lent me two hundred **pounds** d) .... the other day, but I don't know how I can pay him back.

Simon: **Wait a moment**, e) .... there's somebody at the door ... Sorry, Matt, it's Helen. I've got to go.

Matt: OK, **bye** f) ....

Now practise the conversation with a partner.

2 Breaking the news

Imagine you are Matt or Simon. (Remember Simon thinks Melissa is attractive!) You know that Melissa is a terrible singer and you have to tell her gently that she has not got into the band.

Write an SMS to tell her the news or, alternatively, you can ring her up.

Episode 5

Band on the Run.

Before you watch

1 **Would you break the law?**
Read the sentences below and tick (✔) the situations where you would do so.

I would break the law if ...

- my family was in danger.
- I was hungry, and I needed money.
- I thought no one would find out.
- I needed to hide something.
- I didn't agree with the law.
- everybody else did.
- my boss or best friend asked me to.
- I saw an opportunity to make money.
- ....
- ....

Add two more situations.

2 **What are they thinking?**
Use the correct form of the verbs in brackets to complete the characters' thoughts.

If I ....(have) some money, I .... (pay) David back the 200 pounds I owe him. If I .... (impress) Jane with my guitar playing, she .... (like) me again and forget about that annoying American.

If I .... (sing) at the gig, Matt .... (get) the wrong idea about me and him. If Bill .... (see) me with Matt, perhaps he .... (think) I'm only interested in Matt.

(up to **Matt:** *Don't worry!*)

Contract blues

1 Watch ⟩ the section **without sound** and tick (✔) the boxes.

Who looks as if he is:

a) defensive?

   Matt ☐   David ☐   Simon ☐

b) angry?

   Matt ☐   David ☐   Simon ☐

c) offering advice?

   Matt ☐   David ☐   Simon ☐

d) making a demand?

   Matt ☐   David ☐   Simon ☐

Now watch ⟩ again with sound and check.

2 Make sentences. Match the phrases on the left to those on the right.

a) Simon mentions ●

b) Matt is embarrassed about ●

c) David advises them ●

d) Simon tells Matt ●

e) Simon threatens ●

f) Matt tells the others ●

● to follow the contract.

● to do something about it.

● signing the contract.

● not to worry.

● ignoring the contract.

● not to play in the concert.

Now watch ⟩ again and check.

3 **What do you think?**

   • Was it a good idea for Matt to sign the contract?

   • What problem does the band have?

   • Do you think Jane will want to sing in the band?

(up to **Ali**: *It's Eddie.*)

You've got flowers, you've got mail

1 Watch ⟩⟩ the first part of section two (up to **Ali**: *I'll put them in some water*).

What do you think?

- Who are the flowers for?

- Who are they from? Ali says the flowers must be from Bill! Do you agree?

Now share your answers with the rest of the class.

2 Watch ⟩⟩ the second part (up to **Bill**: *Yes!*) Complete the email with suitable words/phrases.

Dear Bill,

I am .... to confirm your promotion to the ....

of Senior Research Manager here in

New York. ....Can.......... you

give me an indication of how soon you

might be able to ....?

I would like you to ......see......

the new position as soon as possible.

Best ....wishes..............,

Donna Shaw
Chief Operating Officer
North American Biotech Inc.

Watch ⟩⟩ again and check.

3 Phrasal verbs with *up*
Watch ⟩⟩ the video (up to **Ali**: *It's Eddie.*).
Complete the spaces, using the verbs in the box.

⋯⋯⋯⋯⋯⋯⋯⋯⋯⋯⋯⋯⋯⋯⋯⋯⋯⋯

come   meet   pick   take

⋯⋯⋯⋯⋯⋯⋯⋯⋯⋯⋯⋯⋯⋯⋯⋯⋯⋯

a) I would like you to .... up the new position as soon as possible.

b) Can we .... up later? Something's .... up, and I'd really like to talk to you about it.

c) I'd rather tell you face to face. I'll ......pick...................... you up at seven. Would that be OK?

SECTION THREE

(up to **Ali:** ... *really change your life?*)

The angry landlord

1 Eddie wants the girls to pay their rent.
   Watch ⫸ the section (up to Eddie walks away) and number
   Eddie's lines in the right order 1 to 5. The first is given.

a) 5 Because if you do that, we'll avoid any unnecessary
       unpleasantness.

b) 3 You're getting behind with your rent and that isn't
       good for anyone.

c) 2 Now listen, girls, I'm a reasonable man, but rules are
       there to be obeyed.

d) 4 Why don't you arrange a standing order with your
       bank to pay me the rent every month?

e) 1 Are you? That's nice.

2 Watch ⫸ the rest of section three and tick (✔) the objects that Matt
   puts in his bag.

3 What do you think?

   • What is Matt going to do? Is he going alone?

SECTION FOUR

(up to **Jane:** *Stop!*)

Breaking and entering

1 Watch ⟫ and tick (✔) the correct answer.

a) Where are Matt and David?

at a café ☐   in a studio ☐   in an office ✔

b) Who does this place belong to?

Bill ☐   Eddie ✔   Helen ☐

c) What are they looking for?

photos ☐   money ☐   document ✔

d) Where is Matt?

near the door ✔   next to a window ☐

in front of David ☐

e) What does Matt do?

He is very careful. ☐   He is very quiet. ☐

He makes a lot of noise. ✔

f) What has David found?

the contract ☐   information on Eddie ✔

suspicious photos ☐

g) What nearly happens to Matt? He nearly gets ...

caught by Eddie. ✔   hit by a lorry. ☐

hit by a car. ✔

Now watch ⟫ again and check.

SECTION FIVE

(to the end of the episode)

Cool, calm and collected

1 **What did they say?** Watch ⟫ the scene and replace the <u>underlined</u> expressions with others actually used by Eddie and David.

Eddie: What <u>are you doing</u> a) *what the hell* .... in here?

David: Legally, it's called breaking and entering.

Eddie: Who <u>are you</u> b) .... ? A lawyer?

David: That's right. And I'm representing Matt and Simon. <u>It's not a good idea to do that</u> c) .... If you call the police, I'll have to show them this ... Mr Usher. Or <u>is it</u> d) .... Mr Pym? Or Mr De Quincey? Or Señor Hector Fernandez? Now, the contract for the band isn't very favourable to my clients. <u>Can I</u> e) .... suggest one or two changes?

2 **Which two things has Eddie agreed to do and what won't he accept?**

He will :

a) ....

b) ....

He won't accept:

c) ....

Watch ⟫ again and check.

Read the summary. It has six mistakes. Correct them.

Simon sent a bunch of flowers to Jane, asking her to be the singer in his band. She thought they were from Bill, but he denied having sent them. He was more worried about his new job promotion in Los Angeles. Meanwhile, Ali tried to persuade Jane not to sing in the band.

David and Matt broke into Eddie Usher's office and found some interesting photos showing Eddie's shady past. They heard Eddie coming, and Matt ran out of the office. Then David confronted Eddie with the evidence and cancelled the contract with him. As Matt ran out of the building, he was almost run over by Jane and Bill who were in Jane's car.

After you watch

1 Write Bill's email replying to his boss about the promotion.

billfisher@northamericanbiotech.com
To: Donna Shaw
Subject: Re: My relocation to N.Y.C

Dear Donna,

Many thanks for

....

....

....

....

....

Bill Fisher
Research Manager
North America Biotech Inc.

Role play

2 Now get into pairs and tell Matt's version of the story.
Student A: You are Jane.
Student B: You are Matt.

Student A: Ask Student B:

Matt, do you mind telling us what's going on?

Listen and ask questions.
For example:
....

Why did you do that?

What happened next?
....

Student B: Tell Jane what has happened.
Mention:

the contract	the flowers	the plan to break into Eddie's office
the break in	the search	Eddie coming
escaping	the car	

Episode 6

The Show Must Go On

Before you watch

1 What do you think?
Think about your favourite song.
Why is it your favourite song?
Is it because of the:

- style (pop, rock, hip-hop, etc.)

- lyrics

- rhythm

- appearance of the singer / group

- speed / tempo

- the fact that your friends like it

- the fact that it's easy to sing

- the memories that it brings

Discuss your reasons with a partner.

2 You receive the following invitation.

CLASS REUNION DINNER

Monday March 29
7.30 p.m. School Hall

followed by ...

KARAOKE NIGHT

Everyone to sing! Decide on your song and ring Maria on 456 567 678 to tell her your choice. Remember each song must be different, so choose two or three in case someone else chooses yours!

PARTNERS WELCOME!

Use vocabulary from exercise 1 to help you explain your choices to the class.

(up to **Ali:** *Well, we've talked about it, that's all.*)

The tenth hour

1 Watch ❯ section one. Are these statements true (T) or false (F)?

a) The postcard is from Matt. ▢

b) It's Saturday. ▢

c) Bill invites Jane for a coffee later. ▢

d) The gig is in 5 hours. ▢

e) David is working for free. ▢

f) Ali thinks Matt is trying to get back together with Jane. ▢

g) Ali is interested in Matt. ▢

2 Now watch ❯ again. Complete Bill and Jane's conversation.

Bill: Jane, hi!

Jane: Oh, hi.

Bill: How're things?

Jane: Oh, fine.

Bill: .... Can we meet up later?

Jane: Uh, I .... I'm not quite sure what I'm doing ...

Bill: ...., I really need to talk to you, and we never really got a chance the other day, what with Matt's unexpected arrival.

Jane: We could talk now.

Bill: ...., I can't right now. I've gotta go to the office.

Jane: On a Saturday?

Bill: There's loads of stuff I need to sort out, ..., for the move back to New York. They're really putting me under pressure to leave as soon as possible.

Jane: Right.

Bill: ...., do you think we could meet up later ... say about eight?

Jane: Well, you can try.

Bill: Don't worry, I will. I'd like to take you out for dinner.

SECTION TWO

(up to Eddie raising his arms in exasperation)

One gig and no singer!

1 **What do you think?**
Watch ❯ the first part of the section (up to Ali shaking her head). Ali seems very interested in Matt. How can we tell? Which of the following do you notice?

- eye contact ∕
- body language ∕
- touch them
- distance between
- laughter ∕
- tone of voice ∕
- silence

2 Watch ❯ the rest of section two.
Who says the following?

a) We're just warming up.

Eddie ☐ Matt ☐ David ☐

b) Where's your singer?

Eddie ☐ Matt ☐ David ☐

c) The contract clearly stipulates that you are not going to sing with the band.

Eddie ☐ Matt ☐ David ☐

d) From a strictly contractual point of view, you're right.

Eddie ☐ Matt ☐ David ☐

e) Eddie, we're on in a few minutes!

Simon ☐ Matt ☐ David ☐

3 **What do you think? Make sentences by choosing the correct phrase on the right.**

a) I was just wondering if ●   ● down to you.

b) She's not ●   ● people from the business.

c) She must have decided to ●   ● going on?

d) OK, Matt. It's ●   ● coming, is she?

e) Can anyone tell me what's ●   ● make it.

f) She couldn't ●   ● there's anything I could do to help.

g) I've invited important ●   ● go out to dinner with Bill.

Now watch ❯ all section two again and check.

37

(up to **Jane:** *... I'm coming!*)

Jane to the rescue

1 Here are three possible dialogues between Bill and Jane.
Which one do you think they say? Why?

a) **Bill:** Jane ... I really love you. You're the most incredible girl I've ever met. I can't live without you.

Jane: That's really sweet of you!

Bill: Will you marry me?

Jane: What?

Bill: Well, I mean ... I don't know what I mean. But I love you and I'll even forget about my work. Please.

Jane: Oh, I'm so sorry! I really ought to answer this.

Bill: OK.

b) **Bill:** Jane ... I really care about you. You're the best thing that's happened to me in a long time and I don't want to lose you.

Jane: Well, I'm not the one who's going to New York.

Bill: You could come with me.

Jane: What?

Bill: Well, I don't mean ... I don't know what I mean. But there must be a way we can make this work. Please.

Jane: Oh, I'm so sorry! I really ought to answer this.

Bill: OK.

c) **Bill:** Jane ... I am really sorry but this isn't working ... I think we should stop before we get hurt. I just don't think I'm ready for a long-distance relationship.

Jane: Was it something I said?

Bill: No ... Not at all. I just don't want to hurt you.

Jane: What?

Bill: I'm sorry. It's been great but I don't think it would work. Please.

Jane: Oh, I'm so sorry! I really ought to answer this.

Bill: OK.

2 Now watch ≫ the first part of the section **without sound** (up to Jane answering the phone). Does your choice fit?

Watch ≫ again with sound and check.

3 Watch ≫ the rest of the section and complete the dialogue.

Ali: Jane, where are you? We need you desperately!

Jane: What's happened?

Eddie: And now let me introduce to you, the one and only Broken Hearts, ... Eddie ... Usher!!!

Jane: Eddie?! ....

Ali: They .... a choice.

Jane: Wait a moment, I need to talk to Bill.

Bill: What's going on? Is it the gig?

Jane: Yeah. It's a disaster. I've really got to go and sing.

Bill: OK! We can .... later.

Jane: Ali ... I'm coming!

Now watch ≫ again and check.

SECTION FOUR

*(up to **Eddie:** ... good deal out of me.)*

Baby please don't go

1 Watch ⟫ and listen to the song *Baby, please don't go.*
Complete the spaces, using the clues in column two.

Baby, please don't go

Baby, please don't go

Baby, please don't go down to (1) ....

You know I (2) .... you so

Baby, please don't go

Baby, your mind done gone

Well, your mind done gone

Well, your mind done gone

Left the (3) .... farm

You got the shackles* on

Baby, please don't go

For be a dog

For be a dog

For be a dog get your way down here

I make you walk the (4) ....

Baby, please don't go

Oh baby, please don't go

(c) J.L. Williams, Universal Music.

* Two metal rings joined together by a chain and placed around prisoners' wrists
or ankles to prevent them from escaping or moving easily

1 Largest city of Louisiana, USA. Famous for Jazz
music.

2 Opposite of *hate*.

3 *Urban* is to *town* as *rural* is to ....?

4 He put the .... on the fire (piece of
wood).

Now watch ⟫ again and check.

2 **What do you think?**
Watch ⟫ the band playing the song with Eddie on vocals.
As you watch, decide if:

a) Eddie is a *good / bad* singer.

b) There are *four / five* musicians.

c) The audience *don't mind / love* the music.

d) Bill *fastens / doesn't fasten* his seatbelt.

e) Eddie is *annoyed / pleased* to see Jane and David.

f) Eddie wishes Jane *good / bad* luck.

SECTION FIVE

(the second song)

Song to the Siren

1 Read the following text.

This song is about the sea. In ancient times, sailors believed there were mythical women called sirens, who were dangerous. This was because when sailors heard them singing, they were so attracted to the voices that they sailed their ships towards them, and entered dangerous waters around the island where the sirens lived. The ships were broken up on the rocks and sank.

Odysseus (Ulysses) is one of the most famous characters in Greek and Roman mythology. On one of his voyages, three sirens tried to attract him and his sailors to their deaths with their melodious voices. However Odysseus was tied to the mast of his ship and his crew filled their ears so they could not hear the singing.

This song is a song to one of the sirens and was first sung by a man, so the 'I' in the song originally refered to a man and the 'you' to a woman.

Song to the Siren by Tim Buckley

Long afloat on **shipless oceans (1)**
I did all my best to smile
'Til your singing eyes and fingers
Drew me loving to your isle (2)
And you sang
Sail to me
Sail to me
Let me enfold you
Here I am
Here I am
Waiting to hold you

Did I dream you dreamed about me?
Were you hare when I was fox? (3)
Now my foolish boat is leaning
Broken lovelorn on your rocks (4)
For you sing, 'Touch me not, touch me not,
Come back tomorrow
O my heart, O my heart shies from the sorrow'

I am puzzled as the **oyster (5)**
I am troubled by the **tide (6)**
Should I stand amidst the **breakers? (7)**
Should I lie with death my bride?
Hear me sing, 'Swim to me, swim to me,
Let me enfold you
Here I am, Here I am, waiting to hold you'

2 Match the images (A) to (G) with the expressions 1 to 7 of the song.

3 Match the word on the left with its definition on the right.

a) shies (vb: *to shy*) • unhappy because the person you love does not love you

b) lovelorn • in the middle of

c) amidst • to turn away suddenly because of fear or surprise

d) enfold • to rest on or against something for support

e) shipless • to surround or enclose somebody / something in your arms

f) lean • (here) no other ship near; alone

g) sorrow • unable to understand something or the reason for something

h) puzzled • a feeling of great sadness

4 Now use all this information to look at the lyrics and answer these questions.

First verse

a) Where was he?

b) What did the siren do?

c) Where is he now?

Second verse

d) *Were you hare when I was fox?* Who is the hunter here?

e) What has happened to his ship?

f) How is he feeling?

Third verse

g) How is he feeling now?

h) What can he do?

i) What does he want?

5 Now watch ≫ and listen to the song on the video.

The Show Must Go On   **41**

Number these sentences 1 to 10 in the order they occur.
The first one has been done for you.

a) 5   Eddie decides to sing.

b) 2   Bill invites Jane out for dinner.

c) 6   Bill tells Jane he doesn't want to lose her.

d) 4   Eddie is angry the band has not found another singer.

e) 1   Matt sends a postcard asking Jane to sing at the gig.

f) 7   Ali phones Jane.

g) 10 The audience love Jane's singing.

h) 8   Jane decides to go to the gig and sing.

i) 3   Ali offers to help Matt at the gig.

j) 9   Eddie gives the microphone to Jane.

Now watch ≫ the whole episode again up to the second song and check.

After you watch

Pairwork
Tim Buckley and Jeff Buckley

Tim and Jeff Buckley were father and son. Both were musicians. Their lives had some similarities and differences.

Student A: Read the biography of Tim Buckley.
Student B: Turn to page 50 and read the biography of Jeff Buckley.

Complete the following information.

Date of birth: ....

Kind of music: ....

First performances: ....

Details of recordings: ....

Age at death: ....

Reason for death: ....

Now exchange this information with your partner and decide how similar and different the information is for father and son.

Tim Buckley was born in February 1947 in Washington D.C., USA. He was a skilled folk singer-songwriter and created subtle intimate music, often with elaborate arrangements. His music consisted of folk-jazz compositions as well as more experimental, free-form work, such as the album *Starsailor*. This later development was not fully understood by all his fans, however. He performed first of all in the folk clubs of Los Angeles and later in bigger venues around the world. A later release of a recording of his 1968 show in London illustrates his impressive creativity.
Sadly, Tim Buckley passed away in June 1975 in Santa Monica, California, USA, the victim of an accidental drug overdose. He was twenty-eight years old.
Reissues of his albums on CD have led to increased interest in his music as did the popularity of his son, Jeff, in the 1990's.
The song *Song to the Siren* appeared on his album *Starsailor* and has been recorded by a number of other artists.

Resource Bank

Episode 1

After watching episode one, choose one of the characters.

You are: ....

You keep a diary. Write about what happened to you and your friends in this episode. Include details about the house-warming party at Jane and Ali's new flat.

June

Sunday 12

	June			
M	•	6	13	20	27
T	•	7	14	21	28
W	1	8	15	22	29
T	2	9	16	23	30
F	3	10	17	24	•
S	4	11	18	25	•
S	5	12	19	26	•

Episode 2

You read the following letters in the 'agony aunt' section of a magazine.

Letter from Helen

I think my boyfriend is losing interest in me. We never seem to have much time to spend together. He always seems to be doing other things. I also do not know what he is doing when he is not with me. If it is so interesting, why doesn't he share it?

I think he might be seeing someone else.

I do not know how long I can carry on like this. It is starting to drive me crazy.

What do you think I should do?

Yours anxiously,
Helen

Letter from Jane

I have recently met a really nice guy, who seems to be really interesting. He is fun and intelligent, and I feel really good when I am with him. I think he is interested in me as well, and I am pretty sure something may happen between the two of us.

The only problem is my ex-boyfriend. I finished our relationship, and he seemed to take it badly. He is very sensitive, and I do not want to hurt him and want us to remain good friends.

What do you think I should do?

Yours hopefully,
Jane

Group B: Write a reply to Jane.

Group A: Write a reply to Helen.

Remember to be sympathetic and offer as much positive advice as you can. You can consider including the following:

- check your own feelings carefully

- be careful not to hurt the other's feelings

- give time to time – do not rush into anything

- talk to friends

Episode 3

Role play

Contract ED

In the episode Simon and Matt say:

Student A:
Imagine you are Simon. You suddenly realize Matt has signed Eddie's contract. Talk to him about it, using the following prompts.

- Talk / David?

- But contract / legal?

- Read it?

- Any more / pages?

- What's in it?

- money / gigs / recordings – obligations?

- If you signed / bad contract / furious!

Student B:
Imagine you are Matt. Simon has realized you have signed Eddie's contract. You do not know the answer to all his questions, so try and be generally positive.

- Oh / David / busy person

- Don't worry / David / check it later

- Well / quickly checked it

- Just one

- Oh the usual. You know …

- Well, gig … yes, er … well, you know …

- No worries. Relax. OK!

Episode 4

Role play

The Dream Band

You work for a record company, Virgo records, and you want to create a pop band to earn you lots of money. Work in groups and choose 4 candidates to make your commercially successful dream band.

Name: Johnny Hall
Age: 21
Hobbies: Dancing and singing.
Experience: None but he studied at the same drama school as Jane.

Name: Suzie Reynolds
Age: 19
Hobbies: Keeping fit and dancing.
Experience: None but she is an excellent dancer. Her friends think she is a terrible singer.

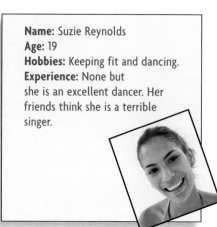

Name: Dave Aplin
Age: 20
Hobbies: Playing the guitar and ... playing the guitar!
Experience: He has played in a few gigs but he is very shy.

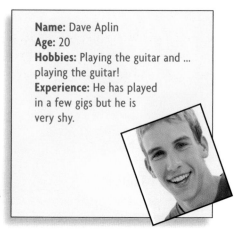

Name: Juliet Lopez
Age: 17
Hobbies: Writing poetry and singing.
Experience: She writes songs and sings in her own band. She has also been a model for 2 years.

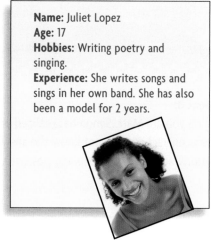

Name: Lucy Bell
Age: 35
Hobbies: Gymnastics and dancing.
Experience: She has been a dancer for many years and has worked with many top bands.

Name: Iggy
Age: 29
Hobbies: Listening to Heavy Metal.
Experience: He is the singer in the rock band *Psychotic Tendencies*.

Name: Julia Smith
Age: 22
Hobbies: Playing the drums and singing.
Experience: She has played many gigs with bands since she was 17.

Name: Carl Beattie
Age: 21
Hobbies: Going out with friends.
Experience: He works as a model and can sing a little.

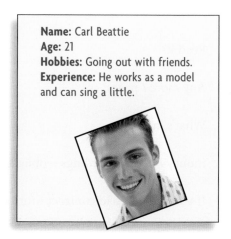

Episode 5

Role play

Sing out sister!

How about trying something that could really change your life?

Student A: Imagine you are Ali.
You really think Jane should sing in Matt's band.
You have promised Matt that you will persuade Jane to sing.
Use these ideas and questions to try and persuade Jane:

- going /sing / band?

- Matt desperate

- Simon / also in band

- Helen and David helping

- Fabulous voice / know songs

- Gig / today!

- Matt knows relationship over

- Talked a lot with Matt

- Agree / Say goodbye

Student B: Imagine you are Jane.
You are not sure about singing in Matt's band.
You have also promised to go out with Bill for dinner.

- Singing? / haven't decided

- Matt / loves me

- Simon in band / pity…

- Yes / my friends too but …

- Thank you but …

- Yes, but / dinner with Bill

- How / know so much?

- OK. Look / in a hurry / talk later?

- Say goodbye

You can use the following language expressions to help you with the role play:

Why don't you …

You really should …

How about …

If you join Matt's band …

Yes, but …

That's all very well, but …

Look, you know that …

Right, but don't you think that …

Take it in turns to be Ali or Jane. Remember you are sisters!

Episode 6

1 All's well that ends well

Now watch  the band perform again. You will see all these
characters in the story.
In the box, make notes on how they are feeling.

WRITE YOUR THOUGHTS HERE

2 The plot continues

Imagine six months have passed. Choose one or more of the following
and decide what has happened to them in this time.

- The Band
- Bill and Jane
- Matt and Ali

- Eddie
- David
- Simon and Helen

Make notes, then present your ideas to the rest of the class.

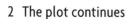

Pairwork

Episode 1

After you watch

Role Play

Student C:

You are Eddie. Show the couple round the flat, using your best 'Eddie' charm! Never admit to any problems!

Use these notes to prepare some answers to possible questions.

- Neighbours / quiet

- Park car / in garden

- Post office / supermarket 100 metres away

- Modern appliances / Central heating

- All bills / extra / Of course!

- Bus no. 43 / to city centre,

- 5 Km to city centre

- No house phone

- Ring me / office hours

- Two months' rent / in advance

Other phrases you may wish to use:

....

What? At this price?

Don't worry about that.

Trust me ... you will love the flat.

....

Episode 2

After you watch

Answers

ABBR.	MEANING	ABBR.	MEANING
AFAIK	As Far As I Know	IOW	In Other Words
ASAP	As Soon As Possible	L8R	Later
ATM	At The Moment	MTE	My Thoughts Exactly
BTW	By The Way	OIC	Oh I See
B4N	Bye For Now	THX	Thanks
CU	See You	U	You
CU L8R	See You Later	U2	You Too
GR8	Great!	U4E	Yours For Ever
IC	I See	WTG	Way To Go!
IMO	In My Opinion	W8	Wait

Episode 6

After you watch

Student B: Read the biography of Jeff Buckley.

Complete the following information.

Date of birth: ....

Kind of music: ....

First performances: ....

Details of recordings: ....

Age at death: ....

Reason for death: ....

Now exchange this information with your partner and decide how similar and different the information is for father and son.

Jeff Buckley was born on 17 November 1966 in Orange County, California, USA and died 29 May 1997 in Memphis, Tennessee, USA. He was the son of the singer-songwriter Tim Buckley, though he did not like to be compared to him. His father had left his mother before he was born.

He studied music at the Los Angeles Musician's Institute, then moved to New York. He played in clubs and coffee houses and was discovered singing his father's song *Once I was* at a tribute concert to his father. He managed to get a record deal with Sony records, releasing the album *Grace*.

His live concerts received great critical acclaim. He had a voice possessing a large vocal range and on stage his vocal performances were described as being spiritual in nature, something unusual in a rock songwriter.

When he was about to resume the recordings for his second album he went for a swim fully clothed in the Mississippi and drowned. He was thirty years old.

Since then, an unfinished album and several live shows have been released in response to the continued interest in his music.

Changing Places

Matt: *Where do you want this chair, Jane? By the window or in the corner over there?*

Eddie: *Ali, it's a lovely flat. And this is a very pleasant street.*

Ali: *What did you say the neighbours were like?*

Eddie: *Oh, don't worry, they're all lovely. You're going to be very happy here. Here, let me give you a hand.*

Matt: *Why did you want to move in here?*

Jane: *I've told you a hundred times, Matt. I needed a change.*

Matt: *But I don't understand. You had a great room at Helen's house.*

Jane: *And more space.*

Matt: *But you haven't got more space here. By the time all your stuff's in, it's going to feel really cramped. And you're moving in with your sister!*

Ali: *This water heater looks a bit old, Mr Usher.*

Eddie: *Call me Eddie.*

Ali: *Is it reliable?*

Eddie: *Reliable? It's top quality, Ali.*

Jane: *I'm sorry, Matt. The whole thing between us was a mistake ... a moment of madness.*

Matt: *It wasn't. I love you.*

Jane: *And I love you, too. But not like that. I think I was feeling sorry for you, and that's not really the basis for a relationship, is it?*

Eddie: *Everything's in perfect working order. Any problems, I'm only a phone call away. Here's my card.*

Ali: *Thanks. But this is only for office hours. Isn't there a twenty-four hour emergency service?*

Eddie: *Ali, do me a favour! On this rent?*

Matt: *Just give me one more chance.*

Jane: *Matt, please ... oh. Oh. Oh no!*

Matt: *That was my fault. I'm really sorry.*

Jane: *No, it wasn't!*

Matt: *Yes, it was!*

Bill: *What the hell's going on down there?*

Jane: *I'm sorry, we just dropped ...*

Matt: *We're just moving in.*

Bill: *Well, can't you move in some other time?*

Matt: *It's two in the afternoon!*

Bill: *I got back from New York at six o'clock this morning! So can you try to keep the noise down?*

Eddie: *Is this your guitar, Jane?*

Jane: *What? No, it isn't.*

Matt: *It's mine. I'm off to a rehearsal now with my band.*

Jane: *I didn't know you were in a band.*

Matt: *Well, you don't know everything about me.*

Jane: *Obviously not.*

Eddie: *You can't judge a book by its cover. Now, I'd like to hear you play. Have you got any gigs planned?*

Matt: *No, we haven't, not yet. We're waiting for the right moment.*

Eddie: *Good for you. I used to be in the music business. I worked with all the biggest bands, Led Zeppelin, Deep Purple, Abba. Maybe I can help you. Has your band made a CD? Here you are, send me a copy.*

Ali: *Oh no! What's happened to our telly?*

Matt: *It was my fault. I dropped it. I'll see if I can get it repaired.*

Eddie: *That's beyond repair, mate.*

Helen: *Professional.*

David: *Non-smoking.*

Helen: *Definitely. What else was in the advert when you moved in?*

Ali: *Here you are.*

Helen : *Oh, thanks, Ali. What time do you finish today?*

Ali: *At six. Are you all coming to see our new flat?*

Helen: *Absolutely.*

David: *Yeah, definitely.*

Ali: *Great.*

Jane: *Quiet.*

Helen: *That's important. Put that in. What is it, David?*

David: *What? Oh, nothing. Just going to the loo. (to Matt) What's going on?*

Matt: *Have you got any money?*

David: *Money? How much? I could possibly manage five pounds.*

Matt: *Two hundred.*

David: *Two hundred pounds?! You must be joking! What on earth do you want two hundred pounds for?*

Matt: *Please, David. It's important. Please!*

Helen: *It's ... nice.*

David: *Is the rent cheap?*

Ali: *Hardly! But the landlord thinks it is.*

Jane: *Well, we are renting the whole flat, not just a room.*

Helen: *Maybe that's Simon.*

Ali: *I'll go.*

Jane: *How are things with Simon?*

Helen: *I don't know. He's always busy. I never see him.*

Jane: *What's that?*

Matt: *I've brought you a house-warming present.*

Jane: *Oh Matt ... it looks really expensive.*

David: *Yes, it cost a fortune.*

Jane: *Simon! Champagne and flowers!*

Simon: *Er ... right.*

Jane: *Thanks, Helen.*

Helen: *That's OK. That was really thoughtful of you.*

Simon: *Yeah, but ... they're not from me. I found them outside the door.*

Ali: *Hang on a sec, there's a note. It's from Bill.*

Helen: *Who's Bill?*

Ali: *'I'm so sorry I was rude earlier. I was really very jet lagged. Welcome to your new home.'*

Jane: *The guy upstairs!*

Matt: *What, that grumpy American?*

Ali: *Well, he can't be that grumpy, can he?*

The American Patient

Jane: *Hi*

Ali: *Hello*

Jane: *See you in a bit.*

Ali: *Yep.*

Jane: *Hi, Helen, I'm so sorry I'm late.*

Helen: *That's all right. Your hair looks wet. I didn't know it was raining*

Jane: It's not. I had a bit of an accident.

Helen: Are you OK?

Jane: Yeah I'm fine; it's a long story. I'll tell you later. But what about you? You sounded really worried on the phone. What's wrong?

Helen: Everything.

Jane: Why?

Helen: Matt's changed since you left. He used to be so quiet, asleep most of the time and half-asleep the rest of it. But now he's taken up the guitar.

Jane: Yeah, he's joined some kind of band, hasn't he? What are they like?

Helen: I haven't heard them. But he's appalling. And I don't know what to do about Simon. It's getting worse. He's just not interested in me anymore. He's always doing something else. Take last Tuesday ...

Helen: ... I'd been waiting outside the cinema for over half an hour before he turned up.

Simon: Hi, pet! Everything all right?

Helen: I was really looking forward to seeing this film. But it had only just started when his mobile rang.

Simon: Hello mate! Wow! OK. Yeah. I'm really sorry, pet, but I've got to go.

Helen: But what about the film?

Simon: Tell me how it ends. I'll call you later.

Helen: It's been like this for weeks. I think he's seeing someone else.

Helen: Are you listening?

Jane: What? That's terrible. You should tell him to turn down the volume.

Helen: Who?

Jane: Matt.

Helen: Matt?! Thanks. That's really helpful. So what happened to you? You said you had some sort of accident.

Jane: Well, it involves our new neighbour.

Ali: Bill, the American?

Jane: Yep.

Helen: Gosh!

Ali: I've got to hear this! I'll be right back.

Jane: Ali had gone to work when I got home. I fancied a relaxing evening, so I made the flat nice and decided to have a shower.

Bill: Are you OK in there?

Jane: Hang on!

Bill: Hello? Is anybody there? Can you hear me? Is everything all right?

Jane: Yes, thank you. I stubbed my toe.

Bill: We haven't been formally introduced. My name's Bill. Bill Fisher.

Jane: And I'm Jane. Jane Wilson. Good to meet you.

Bill: Look, I'm, I'm sorry about the door ... but I, I heard a scream.

Jane: Yeah, it was me. When I got in the shower the water was freezing. I think the water-heater's broken down. You're not an electrician by any chance?

Bill: Well, I am a scientist, although I work in pharmaceuticals, actually. Have you got a screw driver? And a flashlight?

Jane: Oh, you mean a torch.

Bill: Is that what they call it over here?

Jane: Yeah ... but I haven't got one.

Bill: OK, I'll go and get mine. This is appalling. It was put in years ago. Can you turn off the mains switch?

Jane: Er, yeah.

Bill: It's probably in the hall.

Jane: Yeah, right, of course.

Bill: Next to the fuse box ... under the stairs.

Jane: OK. Just as I was going to look for the mains switch the phone rang again. It was you. (To Helen) Hi, Helen. What are you up to?

Helen: I'm standing outside Freud's and waiting for Simon! Can we talk?

Jane: Of course. Shall I come and meet you there, say in half an hour? I'm a bit busy at the moment.

Helen: Thanks, Jane.

Jane: OK. Bye.

Bill: Are you done out there?

Jane: Yep!

Bill: I think I can see the problem! There's a loose wire. Can you hold the ... 'torch' for me?

Jane: Unfortunately ... the electricity hadn't been turned off.

Helen: What do you mean, the electricity hadn't been turned off? You hadn't turned it off!

Jane: I know ... and I felt terrible.

Ali: Was Bill OK?

Jane: Well ...

Bill: Hey, take it easy.

Jane: I am so sorry about this.

Bill: Accidents happen. It's no big deal. But

just wait till I talk to Eddie Usher. That wiring is a disgrace. Ow! What is that stuff?

Jane: It's a homeopathic cure.

Bill: Mmmmm ... unscientific, but it's good. I guess you really like TV.

Jane: Not especially, why?

Bill: Well, that's a pretty impressive screen.

Jane: Oh, that! It was given to me by Matt.

Bill: Is that the guy I saw you with last Sunday?

Jane: Yeah ...

Bill: Is he your boyfriend ?

Jane: No ... ex-boyfriend.

Helen: And then what happened?

Jane: Nothing. I came here and left him to mend the door.

Ali: You didn't?!

Episode 3
The Commitments

Eddie: Nice one boys, very impressive, though you should work on that ending. I've drawn up a contract for you.

Jane: Oh, for heaven's sake!

Bill: Bike trouble?

Jane: Yeah, this old thing's useless. It's such a lovely day, I wanted to go for a ride in the country.

Bill: Well, why don't you come with me? I'm just about to go for a spin in my MG.

Jane: I should stay and sort this out.

Bill: I can fix that for you later. Come on.

Jane: Is that thing safe?

Bill: Safe? You mean like, 'Can it give you an electric shock'?

Jane: I just meant it looks a bit on the antiquated side.

Bill: That is one of the finest sports cars ever made in Britain! So, are you coming?

Jane: OK, have I got time to wash my hands.

Bill: Sure.

Eddie: Cappuccinos all round, Ali! OK, let's get down to business. I liked your CD. I think you boys are good. I even think you might become quite big ... if you get the breaks. But listen, I'm only going to say this once. You must get a new singer. Got it?

Simon: *What's wrong with Matt?*

Eddie: *Do I have to spell it out?*

Matt: *No, don't.*

Eddie: *Good. Because you should always listen to your Uncle Eddie.*

Bill: *So what do you think of my little old English sports car?*

Jane: *I love it.*

Bill: *I never understood why the British stopped making cars. OK, I could understand pulling out of volume production because those cars could be made cheaper elsewhere. But cars for niche markets. The Brits were the best.*

Jane: *Sorry, Bill. This won't take a second.*

Bill: *No problem.*

Jane: *Hi, Helen. It's Jane …*

Eddie: *You don't have to sign anything you don't want to. But if we enter into a formal agreement, I can give you boys a helping hand.*

Ali: *Finished?*

Simon: *Thanks, Ali.*

Matt: *Thanks.*

Simon: *What kind of help?*

Eddie: *First off, I can fix you up with a gig.*

Matt: *A gig?*

Simon: *We could set up a gig for ourselves.*

Eddie: *At The Galaxy? I don't think so.*

Simon: *What else?*

Eddie: *Let's put it this way. I'm seeing an old friend of mine this evening. He signs up new acts for the top record companies. I could ask him to come along to your show. What do you say?*

Jane: *Can you ride?*

Bill: *I may be an American, but I'm no cowboy. I guess you can.*

Jane: *Yeah, I love it. I learned to ride at drama school. It was part of the training. You know: speaking, singing, dancing, horse riding.*

Bill: *Oh, right. So, do you do a lot of acting?*

Jane: *I wish. I actually do a lot of teaching. I've got to make a living.*

Bill: *Sure.*

Jane: *Do you like what you do?*

Bill: *My job? Yeah. The job's good.*

Eddie: *There's no need to read the whole thing. It's a standard agreement.*

Simon: *Sorry. I'll be back in a minute. I just need to have a word with someone.*

Eddie: *Girl trouble?*

Matt: *Mmm.*

Helen: *We're meeting at the Low Bar at about ten, so if you'd like to come along …*

Simon: *Hi, Helen.*

Helen: *Hi, Simon! I didn't see you in here!*

Johnny: *I'll catch you later.*

Simon: *Is he a friend of yours?*

Helen: *Oh yeah. well sort of. Actually, I came in to see Ali. What are you doing here?*

Eddie: *Everything all right? It's all totally above board, Matt. You just have to sign here.*

Matt: *Uh huh. But what about Simon?*

Eddie: *We only need one signature. And your copy. You won't regret this.*

Simon: *You know how Matt's really cut up about Jane. Well, this music thing has become really important to him, and I just wanted to give him some support.*

Helen: *You mean all this secrecy was because of Matt? But why didn't you tell me? I thought that you were seeing somebody else!*

Simon: *I'm sorry. I just didn't think I could tell you. I know you can't stand his music.*

Helen: *That isn't music.*

Simon: *Well, Eddie thinks it is.*

Helen: *And you believe him?*

Simon: *No, but Matt does, and that's enough for me. Where's Eddie?*

Matt: *Oh, he couldn't hang around. He's a busy man!*

Bill: *You know, I haven't had this much fun in a long time.*

Jane: *Me neither.*

Bill: *I'm getting to really like it here.*

Jane: *That's good!*

Bill: *The thing is, I might be going back to the States.*

Jane: *For work?*

Bill: *Yeah. That's why I had to go back to New York, just before you moved into the house. I might be taking on something new. It's not definite. They're still making up their minds.*

Jane: *Hi, Matt. What's up?*

Matt: *Oh, nothing. I was looking for Ali.*

Jane: *She's still at work, isn't she?*

Matt: *Oh, yeah. Right. That doesn't look too good.*

Jane: *Yeah, the chain keeps coming off.*

Matt: *Right. I'll see you then. Bye.*

Jane: *Bye.*

Episode 4
So you wanna be a rock'n'roll star?

Ali: *I'm off. Are you seeing Bill tonight?*

Jane: *Yeah, but just for a drink.*

Ali: *Nothing serious then?*

Jane: *The last thing I need right now is a relationship. Especially one where we could be waving at each other from opposite sides of the Atlantic. He's probably being transferred to New York.*

Ali: *Oh no!*

Jane: *Oh yes … which is why I'm taking a step back.*

Ali: *We should talk about this later.*

Jane: *Yeah, sure.*

Ali: *See you. Bye!*

David: *Oh, sorry … um … I'm a bit lost. I'm trying to find a rehearsal room …*

Melissa: *For 'The Broken Hearts'? Are you going to the audition? You don't look much like a singer.*

David: *Me? No. I'm a friend. A friend and an adviser. Is that where you're going? I can't find the number.*

Melissa: *Me neither. I've never been here before.*

David: *Hang on, I've got an idea.*

Matt: *Hello.*

David: *Hi.*

Matt: *David! Hi! Just a minute, I'm taking a call …*

David: *Matt!*

Matt: *Oh, right. Come in. For the audition?*

Melissa: *Yeah.*

Matt: *Great. We're just this way.*

Jane: *Oh hello. Is that The Cosmic Harmony Centre? Yes, I'm interested in joining one of your tai chi classes. No, I've never tried it. But I do yoga every day.*

Matt: *I'm sure the contract's all right but you know what Helen's like. And she's making Simon nervous, too.*

David: *You know, I'm doing you a big favour here.*

Matt: *Yeah, I really appreciate it.*

David: *I mean, I normally charge for legal advice, and I doubt that you could afford my hourly rate!*

Matt: *And you are...?*

Iggy: *Iggy.*

Matt: *Great! Er ... we're not quite ready at the moment. Why don't you take a seat?*

Iggy: *Whatever.*

Helen: *David, just one thing. It's OK to video the candidates, isn't it?*

Matt: *'Candidates'? It's not a job interview.*

Helen: *David?*

David: *As long as you don't use the video for commercial purposes, it's fine.*

Matt: *That's what I said.*

Helen: *That's brilliant. Thanks for your help, David.*

David: *You know, you still owe me the two hundred pounds I lent you for Jane's TV.*

Matt: *I haven't forgotten it. I'll start paying you back after our gig. You're a real mate!*

Matt: *OK, Melissa, can you tell us something about yourself?*

Melissa: *Sure. Erm, my name's Melissa, but I guess you all know that by now and ... er, I've always wanted to be a singer in a band. In fact, I've been in a band and our records have sold all over the world.*

Matt: *Really?*

Melissa: *You know, I had a number twenty-seven hit in Norway, and got into the top one hundred in Luxembourg. And we were pretty successful for about two years. But then it all went wrong. Our manager was sent to prison ... he was really horrible ... he cheated us out of lots of money.*

Matt: *Uh huh.*

Melissa: *But hey, we were young and innocent. Things happen.*

Helen: *How young?*

Melissa: *Well, I was eight when I joined the band, so I guess I was ten when we split up.*

Matt: *Right. So, could you sing something for us now?*

Melissa: *Sure. I'd love to. I'd like to sing Amazing Grace.*

Melissa: *Amazing Grace, how sweet the sound ...*

Jane: *Hi. Hello, I'd like some information on your acupuncture classes, please ... yeah, it's Jane Wilson. The address is ... number 9, Manchester Road, Oxford ... Ok. Bye.*

Ali: *What do you make of that?*

Jane: *He's amazing. I had no idea he played the piano.*

Ali: *He's quite something, isn't he?*

Jane: *Maybe, but, like I said, he's not for me.*

Ali: *Come off it, Jane! You're crazy about him!*

Jane: *We're just having a bit of fun that's all. We're just two ships passing in the night.*

Ali: *Well, I hope you won't be sending me an SOS!*

Helen: *That was hopeless. Ten singers ...*

Simon: *... and ten disasters.*

Matt: *What about Melissa?*

Helen: *Her singing was even worse than yours!*

Simon: *She's pretty fit though! In an obvious way ... that doesn't appeal to me.*

Helen: *I think we could all do with a drink.*

Matt: *Good idea.*

Bill: *I played in jazz clubs back home. For a time I even thought about going professional, but you know ... work, money, career. Why don't you sing along?*

Jane: *Me?*

Bill: *Why not?*

Jane: *I can't!*

Ali: *You're always singing at home.*

Bill: *Mustang Sally ... Come on. Don't be shy.*

Simon: *Wow!*

Helen: *I think you've found your singer.*

Matt: *Absolutely.*

Simon: *What if Bill doesn't want to do it?*

Matt: *Bill?*

Band on the Run

Simon: *So you're telling us the contract is a disaster.*

David: *I'm afraid so.*

Simon: *What if we decided to ignore the contract?*

David: *Well, you could ignore it, but my advice is that you would be in big trouble.*

Simon: *That's just brilliant! Why did you sign it? A contract drawn up by a wide boy like Eddie Usher!*

Matt: *What happens if we do the gig, David?*

David: *Eddie will get all the money.*

Simon: *I'm not turning up at The Galaxy just to line Eddie Usher's pockets. You'd better do something about that contract. Or we won't be playing any gigs ... anywhere.*

Matt: *OK. I'll think of something.*

Simon: *Yeah right. And what about Jane? Is she going to sing with us or not?*

Matt: *Look. I'm working on it. Don't worry!*

Jane: *Wow! Somebody likes you.*

Ali: *I doubt it.*

Jane: *Who are they from?*

Ali: *I don't know. There's no card or anything.*

Jane: *Oh they're wonderful.*

Ali: *They must be from Bill. He likes to send flowers. I'll put them in some water.*

Bill: *Yes!*

Bill: *Yes! Jane, hi!*

Jane: *Hi, Bill. I don't know what I've done to deserve them but thanks for the flowers.*

Bill: *The flowers?*

Jane: *They're wonderful.*

Bill: *But not from me.*

Jane: *They're not?*

Bill: *No, but anyway, it's good you called. Can we meet up later? Something's come up, and I'd really like to talk to you about it.*

Jane: *Such as?*

Bill: *Well, I really don't want to talk about it on the phone. I'd rather tell you face* to face. I'll pick you up at seven. Would that be OK?

Jane: Sure. See you at seven. Bye! That's weird. They're not from Bill.

Ali: It's Eddie.

Jane: Hello, Eddie.

Ali: We're glad you've called.

Eddie: Are you? That's nice. Now listen, girls, I'm a reasonable man, but rules are there to be obeyed. You're getting behind with your rent and that isn't good for anyone. Why don't you arrange a standing order with your bank to pay me the rent every month? Because if you do that, we'll avoid any unnecessary unpleasantness.

Jane: When you fix the wiring and repair the water heater, we'll pay the rent. But not before!

Ali: That told him. And at least we know Eddie can't have sent the flowers!

Jane: You know what? I think it must have been Matt.

Ali: Perhaps you'd better call him.

Jane: Could you do it? Please?

Matt: Hello, Matt here.

Ali: Is that you, Matt? It's Ali.

Matt: Sorry, Ali. There was, er, something funny with the line.

Ali: I know this is a bit of an odd question ... but did you send some flowers to Jane this morning?

Matt: Will she do it?

Ali: What?

Matt: It was all on the note.

Ali: There was no note.

Matt: Oh no! It must have fallen off. I want her to sing with us.

Ali: Sing with you?

Matt: Well with the band. We need a singer, and when we heard Jane the other night, we thought ... well, I thought she was brilliant.

Ali: Did you? So did I. You know something? That's a really nice idea. I'll have a word with her about it.

Matt: Thanks, Ali. You're a star.

Ali: Bye Matt. How about trying something that could really change your life?

David: I can't believe this. It's crazy. You know I'll lose my job if I get caught.

Matt: Eddie's the real criminal, not us.

David: I'll probably go to prison.

Matt: But if we don't find the contract, I'll never be able to pay you back all your money. So let's get started.

David: Sshhhh! How are we going to find the contract in this lot? It's like looking for ...

Matt: ... a needle in a haystack. I know. Have you got it already?

David: No ... but ...

Matt: It's Eddie.

Bill: So what I wanted to say to you was ...

Jane: They''ve offered you the job in New York.

Bill: That's right. They emailed me this morning and wanted to know how soon I ...

Jane: Stop!

Eddie: What the hell are you doing in here?

David: Legally, it's called breaking and entering.

Eddie: Who do you think you are? A lawyer?

David: That's right. And I'm representing Matt and Simon.

David: I wouldn't do that if I were you. If you call the police, I'll have to show them this ... Mr Usher. Or should I say... Mr Pym? Or Mr De Quincey? Or Señor Hector Fernandez? Now the contract for the band isn't very favourable to my clients. I wonder if I might suggest one or two changes.

Matt: David! Are you OK?

David: Couldn't be better. Listen. Eddie's agreed to make changes to the contract.

Matt: Has he cancelled the gig?

David: No, the gig's fine. Also, he's going to be doing some repairs to Jane's flat. All you need now is a singer.

Matt: A what?

David: A singer!

Matt: Yeah. I'm working on it!

David: Good. The only concession Eddie wasn't prepared to make was that the lead singer could be you. Sorry. Catch you later. Bye.

Matt: Bye.

Jane: Matt, would you mind telling us what's going on?

Episode 6
The Show Must Go On

Matt: I've been dreaming of this, Jane. I always knew you'd come back to me.

Bill: Jane, hi!

Jane: Oh, hi.

Bill: How're things?

Jane: Oh, fine.

Bill: Listen. Can we meet up later?

Jane: Uh, I dunno. I'm not quite sure what I'm doing ...

Bill: The thing is, I really need to talk to you, and we never really got a chance the other day, what with Matt's unexpected arrival.

Jane: We could talk now.

Bill: I'm sorry, I can't right now. I've gotta go to the office.

Jane: On a Saturday?

Bill: There's loads of stuff I need to sort out, you know, for the move back to New York. They're really putting me under pressure to leave as soon as possible.

Jane: Right.

Bill: Anyway, do you think we could meet up later ... say about eight?

Jane: Well, you can try.

Bill: Don't worry, I will. I'd like to take you out for dinner.

Ali: I've been thinking.

Jane: Oh oh.

Ali: No, really. What are you going to do about the band?

Jane: Oh, don't you start. I've already been sent this. He's a bit desperate, isn't he?

Ali: Well, wouldn't you be? The gig's in ten hours. You've got to let him know.

Jane: I will, I will.

Ali: It'd be awful to let him down. And it isn't just him. There's Simon. There's Helen, she's doing everything she can. Even David's helping out ... and for no money! Why don't you sing with them? You know the songs, and you've got a fabulous voice. What have you got to lose?

Jane: You know what the problem is. I just don't want Matt getting the wrong idea. Anyway, Bill wants to take me out for dinner tonight. Funny how people think bad news and food go together.

Ali: *I really think you should give Matt a break. Doesn't he deserve it?*

Jane: *Deserve it?*

Ali: *He's put such a lot of effort into this band. And he's tried so hard to put your relationship behind him. He isn't trying it on, I'm sure of it. He doesn't want to get back together with you.*

Jane: *You seem to know an awful lot about Matt all of a sudden.*

Ali: *Well, we've talked about it, that's all.*

Matt: *One, two. One, two.*

Ali: *It's not very original!*

Matt: *Ali! It's great to see you, but you're a bit early for the gig.*

Ali: *I know … I was just wondering if there's anything I could do to help.*

Matt: *That's really nice of you.*

Ali: *Well, I want it to go well.*

Matt: *Is there any news about Jane?*

Jane: *Hi.*

Bill: *Hi.*

Matt: *She's not coming, is she?*

Ali: *She must have decided to go out to dinner with Bill.*

Simon: *OK, Matt. It's down to you.*

Eddie: *Can anyone tell me what's going on?*

Matt: *We're just warming up.*

Eddie: *Where's your singer?*

Matt: *She couldn't make it.*

Eddie: *Couldn't make it? I've invited important people from the business. I've signed a contract that gives away nearly all my rights, and now you're telling me you haven't even got a singer. You're not singing, Matt. No way. The contract clearly stipulates that you are not going to sing with the band. Am I right or am I right?*

David: *From a strictly contractual point of view, you're right.*

Matt: *Eddie, we're on in a few minutes!*

Bill: *Jane … I really care about you. You're the best thing that's happened to me in a long time. And I don't want to lose you.*

Jane: *Well, I'm not the one who's going to New York.*

Bill: *You could come with me.*

Jane: *What?*

Bill: *Well, I don't mean … I don't know*

what I mean. But there must be a way we can make this work. Please.

Jane: *Oh I'm so sorry! I really ought to answer this.*

Bill: *OK.*

Ali: *Jane, where are you? We need you desperately!*

Jane: *What's happened?*

Eddie *And now let me introduce to you, the one and only Broken Hearts, featuring … Eddie … Usher!!!*

Jane: *Eddie?! You've got to be joking!*

Ali: *They didn't have a choice.*

Jane: *Wait a moment, I need to talk to Bill.*

Bill: *What's going on? Is it the gig?*

Jane: *Yeah. It's a disaster. I've really got to go and sing.*

Bill: *OK! We can sort this out later.*

Jane: *Ali … I'm coming!*

Eddie: *Baby, please don't go*
Baby, please don't go
Baby, please don't go
Down to New Orleans
You know I love you so
Baby please don't go

Baby, your mind done gone
Well, your mind done gone
Well, your mind done gone
Left the country farm
You got the shackles on
Baby, please don't go

For be a dog
For be a dog
For be a dog
Get you way down here
I make you walk the log
Baby, please don't go

Oh baby, please don't go

Eddie: *What's up? What's going on?*

Matt: *Sorry, Eddie. Change of plan.*

Eddie: *What's she doing here? The contract clearly stipulates …*

David: *… that the band can choose its own singer. Provided it's not Matt. Come on, Eddie. You know it makes sense.*

Eddie: *Break a leg! You'd better be good. Those boys have got a damn good deal out of me.*

Jane: *Long afloat on shipless oceans*
I did all my best to smile
'Til your singing eyes and fingers
Drew me loving to your isle
And you sang
Sail to me
Sail to me
Let me enfold you
Here I am
Here I am
Waiting to hold you

Did I dream you dreamed about me?
Were you hare when I was fox?
Now my foolish boat is leaning
Broken lovelorn on your rocks
For you sing, 'Touch me not, touch me not, come back tomorrow
O my heart, O my heart shies from the sorrow'

I am puzzled as the oyster
I am troubled by the tide:
Should I stand amidst the breakers?
Should I lie with death my bride?
Hear me sing, 'Swim to me, swim to me, let me enfold you
Here I am, here I am, waiting to hold you'